FUNNY POEMS
For CHRISTMAS

Christmas Alphabet

abcdefghijkmnopqrstuvwxyz

(NO EL)

Liz Brownlee

Other fantastic poetry
collections from Scholastic:

Disgusting Poems
Magic Poems
Animal Poems
Pet Poems
School Poems
Spooky Poems
Funny Poems
Family Poems
Silly Poems
Dinosaur Poems

FUNNY POEMS
FOR CHRISTMAS

Compiled by
Paul Cookson

Illustrated by
Sarah Nayler

■SCHOLASTIC

For Paul, Helen, Harriet and Chloe

Special thanks to: Ella, Sam, Daisy, Sally, Lydia,
Emma and Ben for your speedy Christmas poems. Thanks for
responding so quickly under
pressure – sorry they couldn't all go in.

First published in the UK by The Book People Ltd in 2005
This edition published by Scholastic Ltd, 2006
Scholastic Children's Books
An imprint of Scholastic Ltd
Euston House, 24 Eversholt Street
London, NW1 1DB, UK
Registered office: Westfield Road, Southam, Warwickshire, CV47 0RA
SCHOLASTIC and associated logos are trademarks and
or registered trademarks of Scholastic Inc.

10 digit ISBN 0 439 95049 X
13 digit ISBN 978 0439 95049 7

Clubs and Fairs 10 digit ISBN 0 439 94410 4
Clubs and Fairs 13 digit ISBN 978 0439 94410 6

Printed and bound by Nørhaven Paperback A/S, Denmark
Papers used are made from wood grown in sustainable forests

1 3 5 7 9 8 6 4 2

www.scholastic.co.uk/zone

CONTENTS

Boxing Day Blues and Christmas Thank Yous

Last Word

Acknowledgements

First Word

O, Merry Be, Both One And All

O, merry be, both one and all
This festive Christmas season
Let stockings hang from every wall
With joyful hope and reason
As family and friends do call
May company be pleasing
And let the snowflakes gently fall
This festive Christmas season

O, celebrate in revelry
Now Yuletide has begun
Sing carols' holy melody
The Virgin Mary's son
And look ahead at what's to be
And what is yet to come
'Tis a time of mystery
Now Yuletide has begun

Saint Nicholas attired in red
Now Christmastime is here
With reindeers seven before his sled
This one night of the year
All children good tucked up in bed
Dreams of gifts that cheer
So onward let us all be led
Now Christmastime is here

God bless all merry gentlefolk
It's Christmas! Let us shout!
Uncork the wine and laugh and joke
Let love and joy ring out
Sing on until our voices croak
While snow be round about
May sleigh day dreams be filled with hope
It's Christmas! It's Christmas!
IT'S CHRISTMAS! Let us shout!

Neville Ambrose Xavier

Away in a Manger

Something to Play With

I told my brother Ben
who is younger than me
part of the Christmas story
and he said worriedly
"did no one bring the baby
a toy or teddy bear
or something to play with?
What could he do with myrrh?"
Ben thought myrrh sounded horrid,
he thought the same of frankincense;
in fact Ben thinks that Jesus
did badly over presents

Peggy Poole

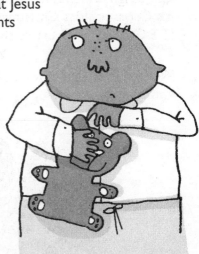

Stable Song

She lies, a stillness in the crumpled straw
Whilst he looks softly on the child, unsure,
And shadows waver by the stable door.

The oxen stir; a moth drifts through the bare
Outbuilding, silken Gabriel-winged, to where
She lies, a stillness in the crumpled straw.

A carpenter, his wife, both unaware
That kings and shepherds seek from them afar
And shadows waver by the stable door.

The child sleeps on. A drowse of asses snore;
He murmurs gently, raises eyes to her
Who lies, a stillness in the crumpled straw.

A cockerel crows, disturbed by sudden fear
As shepherds, dark upon the hill, appear
And shadows waver by the stable door.

The hush of birth is in the midnight air
And new life hides the distant smell of myrrh;
She lies, a stillness in the crumpled straw,
And shadows waver by the stable door.

Judith Nicholls

Nativity in 20 Seconds

Silent night
Candle light
Holy bright

Stable poor
Prickly straw
Donkey snore

Babe asleep
Lambs leap
Shepherds peep

Star guide
Kings ride
Manger side

Angels wing
Bells ring
Children sing
WELCOME KING!

Coral Rumble

What Christmas is for

Christmas is a time for gifts –
For giving and for getting.

Christmas is a time for peace –
Forgiving and forgetting.

Philip Waddell

The Shepherd's Story

Snow.
Just as it was growing dark – snow.
Soft flakes fell
White and glossy
Thick as swans' feathers
Slowly, slowly,
Until the world was put to bed
Under this white quilt
Slowly slowly drifting
Into sleep …
Then. In that silence
The sky was suddenly alive
With angels bright as fire
Their wings burning with such golden light
Their songs like thunder and like ice,
Like bells and like the deep and sonorous sea.
Their message stranger
Than any other I have ever heard.
"God is born," they said.
"The God who spoke and shaped the world
The stars, the universes
And the soft black deeps of space
Is born."
There on that hillside
In that snow
I heard them say it.
Then just as quickly they were gone

The sky was dark again
No echo lingered
Nothing
But the white white snow
The secret white white snow
Nothing has ever been a greater mystery
Than that night.
With angels. Snow.
A million different kinds of light
I knew then that the world is not an ordinary place
When heaven shone from one small baby's face.

Jan Dean

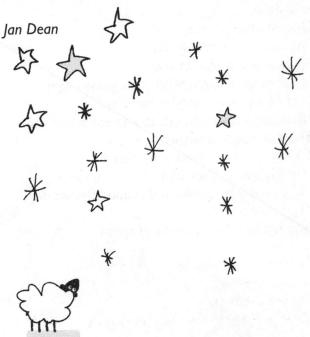

Who Was There?

Who was there that first Christmas day?
Who saw the baby lying in the hay?

"I," said the cow with the crumpled horn,
"I was there when the baby was born."

"I," said the owl, "from my perch up high,
I heard the baby give his first cry."

"I," said the spider, "as I spun my thread,
I saw Mary stroke the baby's head."

"I," said the donkey, "I was there.
I saw the shepherds kneel in prayer."

"I," said the sheep, "I saw the star
And followed the wise men from afar."

We all were there that first Christmas day.
We saw the baby asleep in the hay.

John Foster

WANTED

WANTED: a reliable STAR
to lead small party westwards.
Bright with good sense of direction.
No timewasters.
Send CV to CHILDTREK, EARTH.

Sue Cowling

Saturday Night at the Bethlehem Arms

Very quiet really for a Saturday.
Just the old couple come to visit relations
Who took the double room above the yard
And were both of them in bed by half past nine.
Left me with that other one, the stranger.
Sat like he was set till Domesday at the corner of
   the bar
Sipping small beer dead slow and keeping mum,
Those beady, tax-collector's eyes of his
On my reflection in the glass behind the bar
Watching me, watching me.
And when he did get round to saying something
His talk was like those lines of gossamer
That fishermen send whispering across the water
To lure and hook unwary fish.
Not my type. And anyway I'd been on the go
   since five.
Dead beat I was.
Some of us have a bed to go to, I thought to myself.

Knock Knoc

I was just about to call Time
When the knock came at the door.
At first I was for turning them away;
We only have two rooms see and both of them
  were taken.

But something desperate in the woman's eyes
Made me think again and I told them,
They could rough it in the barn
If they didn't mind the cows and mules for
  company.
I know, I know. Soft, that's me.

I yawned, locked up, turned out the lights,
Rinsed my hands to lose the smell of beer.
Went up to bed.
A day like any other.
That's how it is.
Nothing much ever happens here.

Gareth Owen

Letters and Wish Lists

Dear Santa, Here's my Christmas List

Dear Santa, here's my Christmas list.
I hope you'll bring it all.
I've only asked for gifts my parents
can't find at the mall.

I'd like to have a UFO,
with aliens inside,
and maybe a Tyrannosaurus Rex
that I could ride.

A ninety-nine foot robot
is a present I could use.
I'll also need a time machine,
and rocket-powered shoes.

Please bring a gentle genie
who will grant my every wish,
and don't forget a wizard's wand,
and, yes, a talking fish.

Of course, I'll need a unicorn,
and won't you please provide
a dragon, and a castle
in the English countryside.

But if the weight of all these things
might cause your sleigh to crash,
I'll understand. If that's the case,
dear Santa, just bring cash.

Kenn Nesbitt

Take Note...

I emailed Father Christmas
At santaclaus.com
With this year's Christmas list
And everything I want
Expensive and expansive
I asked for such a lot
Then Santa emailed back
And this is what I got
A print out of another list
Of things that I should leave
At the bottom of the chimney
On this Christmas Eve...
Snow proof leather Wellingtons
Thermal underwear
Gloves with fleecy lining
A hat that's lined with fur
A scarf that's extra long
To wrap around a beard of white
Goggles for the snowstorms
Headlights for the stormy night
Reindeer socks and woolly hats
Carrots, milk and oats
Sherry, pies and whisky
To warm up winter throats
Chocolate bars for energy
Coffee, tea and cake
Matchsticks to help tired eyes

To try and stay awake
It finished with a little note
From Santa Claus himself
Wishing us the very best
Happiness and health
I read it once then once again –
Seeing is believing –
He said "Remember ... Christmas is
For giving, not receiving"

Paul Cookson

Please Don't

Dear Santa,

Please don't leave underwear,
neckties, or socks.
And I am too old, now,
for marbles and blocks.

Don't leave me anything
purple or pink.
And I have moved way beyond
board games, I think.

Footballs or cricket bats
are mainly moronic,
unless you can make them
more electronic.

Please don't bring anything
I've got to make.
And things that are fragile
I'll probably break.

Don't leave me trousers,
or starchy bright shirts.
Your taste is appalling;
and the teasing? It hurts.

I'm tired of presents
I've already got.
I'm sorry to sound like I'm whining.
I'm not.

But, I knew it might help you
to know what I hate.
So, just about anything else
would be great!

Ted Scheu

Welcome Note

Dear Santa, welcome to our house.
Sorry there's no chimney for you but
a patio door is much less sooty
don't you think?

Please make yourself at home.
Sit down and drink
a modest medium sherry once again.
Try not to let it dribble down your chin;
it marked the table last year (note the stain).

I baked the mince pies fresh today.
Have one or two, but there again take care –
I want No Crumbs, because, you see, last year,
regretfully, I found them everywhere.

You'll find the children's stockings by their beds.
Be more sensible than usual – nothing loud.
No monkey this time please, or anything
that makes a mess.

I hope you've read the notice on the door
and left your boots out on the patio. Last year –
Muddy Footprints Everywhere.
All Christmas Day I scrubbed the carpet but
if you look closely you'll see they're still there.

Last, and I most sincerely hope you'll pardon
any offence this causes them, but reindeer
aren't the most fastidious of eaters are they?
I must insist they crunch their carrots
   IN THE GARDEN.

So make yourself at home, be of good cheer.
Thanks for coming.
Have a lovely year.

Frances Nagle

Dear Santa

Please can I have an elephant?
We could keep it in the garage.
I will use my pocket money
To buy bales of straw.

Oh, please, please can I have an elephant?
No matter what my mum said.
She is good with animals
And I am sure she'll be OK with it
Once the shock's worn off.

I need this elephant.
I need to ride it down the street,
My legs tucked in behind its flapping ears.
I need to tie it to the railings outside school.
Please, please, dear Santa,
Let me have an elephant
Then everyone will want to sit with me
And share my stuff
And I will never have to be
The one left out.

Jan Dean

Christmas Wish

Dear Father Christmas,
I have seen
other children on TV
who are thin and hungry
not lucky like me.
Please will you give
my presents to them?
I don't know how
to send them you see.

Lynne Taylor

Dear Santa...

I'm writing you this little note
just to say hello.
It's Christmas Eve. I'm in bed, but
I just want you to know
that what I'd like for Christmas is ...
some snow.

Can you do it? Can you try?
Dad says you're really clever.
And I'll leave you a fresh mince pie
and carrots for Rudolf for ever
if, on Christmas Day there's Christmas ...
weather.

I don't want other prezzies,
no board-games, toys or clothes.
But if you've got some sledges,
could you please leave one of those,
so I'm good and ready when ...
it snows.

Just enough snow for a snowman
and to have a snowball fight,
and by tomorrow morning.
Oh, and the sledge. All right?
Happy Christmas, Santa. Lots of love …
night, night.

David Horner

A Christmas Booklist

The Christmas Story by Wayne A Manger

Give Us A Kiss by Miss L Toe

Opening Your Presents by Russell O'Paper

HEAVENLY MUSIC? BY CAROLE SINGERS

Time Uncle Jim Was Going by Wenceslas Bussom

SEASON'S GREETINGS BY MARY CHRISTMAS

The Inedible Vegetable by Bruce L Sprout

Overcooked by Bern Toffering

A Perfect Picture of Christmas by Robin and Holly Bush

How To Stuff A Turkey by Phyllis Cavity

Santa's Favourite by Sherri and Min Spies

A COLLECTION OF CORNY JOKES BY PAUL A CRACKER

WE'VE EATEN TOO MUCH BY IVOR PAYNE AND BEN TOVER

Is Christmas Finished? by Shirley Knot

Trevor Parsons

Drawback

The fairy on top of the Christmas tree
Said, "I hate my job, it's rotten –
How would you like it, perched up here
With pine needles stuck up your bottom?"

Clive Webster

Home-made Cards

Making Christmas cards at home
Is difficult to do –
You need some scissors of your own
And lots and lots of glue.

You need some stars upon the front
Or else they will be dull,
And you can make a snowman too
From balls of cotton wool.

You'll need your crayons – green for trees
And red for Rudolph's nose,
And gold to light a candle up
So that it really glows.

Now sprinkle over everything
(Plus house and babysitter)
The final, most important thing –
Lots and lots of glitter.

Clare Kirwan

36

Christmas Tree

My
dad's
got an
allergy
to Christmas
trees – no honestly
they make him sneeze –
and scratch and sniff and his
eyes all run – so Christmas time
was
not
much
fun
– until we
bought a
plastic one

James Carter

Chrismixed-up Mum

Mum's had too much sherry
With all the preparations
She seems to be mixed up
With Christmas decorations

The tree is in the bath
There's tinsel in the street
There's crackers in the shed
And holly on the toilet seat

Streamers on the garden fence
Stockings on the dog
And mistletoe on the chimney
So Santa gets a snog!

Paul Cookson

38

Christmas Tingle

The word
"Christmas"
is made of silver,
tinsel fine.
Hanging
on a Christmas tree
it tinkles
like the tiny bells
of a wind-chime,
twinkles
like excitement.
Sparkles.
Like magic.

Lynne Taylor

Remember to Wrap the Presents

Turkey, plum-pudding, brandy, mince-pies,
Crackers, tinsel, the Christmas tree,
Presents, charades, chocs, pantomime,
Everyone's thanked but me.

When it comes to good wishes, I'm forgotten,
Bundled away in the dark.
But without me your Christmas stuff looks rotten,
And usually falls apart.

Spare us a thought: accept our good wishes;
Remember, we keep things in shape.
Love from the cardboard boxes, the tissue
Paper …
    and me, your sellotape.

Leo Aylen

Deck the Halls

Deck the halls with boughs of holly
La la la la la di dah di dah
I saw Daddy kiss Aunt Molly
La la la la la di dah di dah
Mummy hit him with her brolly
La la la la la di dah di dah
Then he didn't look so jolly
La la la la la did dah did dah

Roger Stevens

Christmas Baubles

Baubles
fragile, fire-bright
hanging, hovering, quivering
reflectors of tiny glinting tints
tree treasures

Kate Williams

Funny Family Gatherings

Family Christmas Scene

Sister is an angel
Mummy is a fairy
Grandma is our Santa –
She's old and white and hairy

Paul Cookson

Christmas Invitation

Sally had an elephant
Soft and pink and blue,
Auntie had a petticoat
And Arthur had the 'flu.

Janice had a pretty hat
Friskie had a bone,
Granny had a headache
And Uncle had a moan.

Billy had a bellyache
The salmon tasted tinned,
Bertie had an argument
And Walter had the wind.

Minnie had a nasty turn
Mother had a weep,
Uncle had the whisky
And Auntie fell asleep.

Colin had a hacking cough
Cathy had a fit
Uncle had tummy ache
And the baby had a nit.

Mildred had lie-down
The telly got the blink,
Auntie made a trifle
And Uncle made a stink.

Mavis had a big "to do"
– Someone squashed her hat,
Auntie saw the future
And Uncle saw a rat.

Frankie had a funny knee
Daisy had a corn,
Bob had awful rumbles
And Harry had the yawns.

Oh, we had a lovely Christmas
Relations are such FUN...

So here's an

Invitation

Next year ...
Yes ...

You can come!

Clive Webster

Christmas is Coming

Christmas is coming
we're going to granny's flat,
let's hope she doesn't
wear that flowery hat
or overcook the turkey
or serve up Brussels sprouts.
And if she makes us watch the Queen
I'm organizing a walk out!

Rupert M Loydell

Family Get-together

Doorbell ringers
Arm flingers.
Present bringers
Round the piano singers.
Fast talkers
Room to room walkers.
Channel switchers
Skirt hitchers.
Line dancers
Daft Dad prancers.
Balloon bouncers
Surprise pouncers.
Computer game players
Baddie slayers.
Meat eaters
No one's plate – is piled higher – than Uncle Peter's!
Beer swillers
Story tellers.
Joke sayers
Auld Lang Syne swayers.
Arm linkers
Champagne drinkers.
Party ravers
Hometime wavers.

Lisa Watkinson

Barely Worth It

Relatives descend.
Wet kisses and questions are
the price of presents.

Ted Scheu

Star Worms

At Christmas
We play charades
Granny puts up three fingers
And says, Six syllables
And we say, That's three
She points at her nose
Pulls her ear and goes boss-eyed
Jumps up and down
Does a wavy thing
With her arms
That looks like she's praying
Or swimming
And we try to guess and she says
Star Worms

Roger Stevens

Christmas

My dad says
Christmas is like snow:
Exciting
When you're little,
But a bind
Once you've grown up.

My grandad says
That that just means
He's jealous of me
And my sledge.

Kevin McCann

After-dinner Sleep

Asleep in her armchair
Great, Great Granny grumbles
plays musical tummies
with gurgles and rumbles,

she splutters her way through a chorus of snores
that rattle her teeth like an old dinosaur's
then shudders as sherry is regurgitated
and burps with such gusto her stomach's deflated.

Asleep in her armchair
Great, Great Granny grumbles
plays musical tummies
with gurgles and rumbles.

Gina Douthwaite

Things I Don't Want to Meet Under the Mistletoe

Nana and her false teeth!
The smelly garlic breath emanating from Uncle
  Keith!

Grandad's whiskers – sharp and long
Auntie's perfume – far too strong!

Mum and her lipstick – red and smudgy
A little sharp peck from Casper the budgie

Grandma and her facial hair
Her moustache will give you a scare!

Dad's beard full of last night's cheese
Beans, chips and mushy peas

The cat's pink tongue, its sandpaper lick
Its giant furballs make me sick!

The snog of the dog – all slimy and blubbery
Its dribbling tongue – pink and rubbery!

Sister's smile smothered in gravy
I tell her she's being crazy!!!

Sam Cookson
Aged 12

Parties, Crackers and Corny Jokes

Christmas Crackers (Cheapo Selection Box)

CRACK!

One paper hat.

One plastic toy
(which, inevitably, snaps).

One riddle:
What are Santa's Arctic helpers called
who don't have any underwear?

Polar bares!

Mike Johnson

What a Lovely Party

The Christmas party was in full swing
Down at the Youth Club hall –
Spirits were high and laughter was loud,
With everyone having a ball.

Food and drinks were plentiful,
The disco music loud,
Youngsters all enjoying themselves,
A happy Christmas crowd.

But the dance floor space was very small,
There was treading on people's toes,
And if you waved your arms around
You'd catch somebody's nose.

And really, that's what started it –
Little Jimmy Mann
Caught Lucy Snodgrass on her snitch,
And then the war began.

Lucy grabbed the nearest trifle
And pushed it in his face,
And that was the cue for everyone
To set about the place.

Custard creams zoomed through the air,
Vanilla ices flew,
Walnut whips and chocolate drops
And a hot mince pie or two.

Sausage rolls and sandwiches,
Celery sticks and dips,
Sardines and tomatoes,
Pork pies, crisps and chips.

Kids were covered head to toe,
Hair was soaked and matted,
The floor was just a sea of food,
The walls and windows splattered.

And when it finally ended,
It looked like World War Three,
Then the Youth Club Leader popped inside –
"Have you enjoyed your tea?"

But when her eyes took in the mess
She said, "Oh dear, oh dear.
You naughty, naughty children –
There'll be no food next year!"

Clive Webster

Six Economy Christmas Crackers

This joke fell out when the cracker went **PHUT**
With a little plastic Noddy –
What was The Snowman before he found fame?
Answer: Just a snowbody.

This joke tipped out when the cracker went **RIP**
With a silver gilt horseshoe –
What does Santa use to fix broken toys?
Answer: A spot of Super Igloo.

This joke dropped out when the cracker went
With a dinky Alice band –
CRUMP
Where do cats take winter breaks?
Answer: Where else … Lapland!

This joke spilled out when the cracker went **TEAR**
With a metal thing to clack –
Why does Rudolph pull Santa's sleigh?
Answer: It's either that or the sack!

This joke slipped out when the cracker went **SPLIT**
With a boot for a tiny foot –
What does Santa wear to deliver gifts?
Answer: His two piece soot.

This joke popped out when the cracker went **PUFF**
With a novelty keyring – joy!
Is Santa's wife older or younger than him?
Answer: Older. (He's a toy boy!)

Philip Waddell

Crackers!

This Christmas cracker just won't crack
I've pulled it this way, pulled it that
I've squashed it, squeezed it, pressed it flat
But I don't seem to have the knack
To make this Christmas cracker crack.

... So just take that you cracker!

WHACK!

Mary Green

Silent Nightmare

There's a loud party in the kitchen –
My sisters are having a fight.
Auntie bought me a set of drums
And I'm playing "Silent Night".

Bill Condon

Some Truthful Answers to Well-Known "Mottos" Found in Christmas Crackers

What did the earwig say
When it fell off the branch of a tree?
("YA-AA-AH-HH…!"
Then – soon after – *"Splat!"*)
Why did the chicken cross the road?
(Because it got chased by a cat.)
When is a door NOT a door?
(That's easy! When it's a wall…)
And what did the big chimney say to the little?
("Chimneys" *don't* speak at all!)

Trevor Harvey

Christmas Crackers

I rattle the cracker to my ear
When it's pulled what will appear –
A riddle, a whistle, a paper hat?
The contents will bore me, that's a fact

Last year my hat split on my head
And my riddle was stupid it must be said
– What goes up when the rain comes down? –
And a plastic ring the worst in town

But still every year the crackers are placed
We all know this moment must be faced
But though I pretend it's really fun
I'm hungry for my dinner so let's get it done

Janet Greenyer

A Christmas Riddle

My first is in icing, mincemeat and spice
My second's in sherry and there appears twice
My third lies in brandy but not wine or beer
And my fourth is in socks which my dad gets
   each year
My fifth hides in stocking which hangs by your bed
My sixth's seen in present and also in sled
My last's found in robin and also in tree
I help to make Christmas but what could I be?

Answer: CRACKER

62

Festive Food

Reggie

A very fat turkey named Reggie
At Christmas became rather edgy,
He was huffin' and puffin'
At the mere thought of stuffin'
– How he wished everyone was a "veggie".

Colin West

Christmas Stuffing

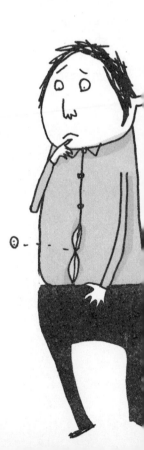

Auntie, Auntie
For heavens sake
Give us all
a bit of a break!
I sure don't need another
piece of Christmas cake.

I'm stuffed already
don't need any more
can't get up
can't get through the door
want to lie
down flat
want to
fall in a heap
want to
close my eyes
and go to sleep!

Yeah, Christmas wishes
and Christmas Greetings ...
... but it seems to me
I spend all Christmas
EATING!

Trevor Millum

Sing a Song of Christmas...

Sing a song of Christmas,
how we hate mince pies:
four-and-twenty cold ones
left in a pile.
When the hols are over
they go back in the tin
and several weeks later
are thrown into the bin.

Rupert M Loydell

Turkey Surprise

Now Christmas lunch is quite a treat
With crackers, hats and lots to eat
But every year mum buys a bird
The size of which is quite absurd.

Fifteen pounds of turkey meat
Is far too much for three to eat
Yet every year she does the same
She plays her outsized turkey game.

Now as I've said it's quite a treat
This splendid lunch with lots to eat,
But that which follows makes us cringe
It's mother's five day turkey binge.

There's turkey rissoles, turkey stew,
Turkey broth and curry too
Turkey burgers, cold turkey thighs
Not to mention turkey surprise.

Now come on mum, enough's enough!
We've had our fill of turkey stuff
Please listen to us, mother dear,
And buy an eight pound bird next year.

Richard Caley

Christmas Dinner

"We had my Granny for Christmas,"
Remarked little Jimmy to Ed.
"Really? Hey, that's wicked,
We just had turkey," Ted said…

Clive Webster

Christmas Dinner

Ahh, what a feast
Boiled to bits Brussels
Cracking crackling
Don't forget the dog
Extra bread sauce?
Fancy some ham?
Gallons of gravy
Hurry up while it's hot
I want some more...
Jugs of juice
Kilos of carrots (and potatoes and parsnips and...)
Lots of leftovers
Many more mince pies
No more for me...
Oh, go on
Piles of puddings
Quite a lot of custard please...
Right, that's it, stop there
So many sweets
Those are my favourites
Up for more? Was it good?
Very nice, thanks but I'm full...
Well, just a little Wensleydale

Xtra After Eights?
Your turn to wash up
Zzzzzzz after lunch

Suzanne Eldvidge

My Mince Pies (Keep Off)

By the light of the lights
Of the Christmas tree,
The pies on this plate
Are all for me.

And if anyone tries
To pinch my mince pies,
They dies, they dies,
If they touches my pies.

I know Christmas time
Is a time to be kind,
So I'm nice as can be,
But there's one thing I mind…

And that's if anyone tries
To pinch my mince pies,
So keep *your* hungry eyes
Off of *my* mince pies.

I don't care who you are
– Even Santa Claus.
Just keep away
With your thieving paws!

'Cos if anyone tries
To pinch my mince pies,
They dies, they dies,
If they touches my pies.

It's not that I'm greedy.
I'm nice as can be.
But the pies on this plate
Are *all* for me.

David Bateman

Festive Question

Turkey-minder,
Bacon-rinder,
Parsnip-chipper,
Sherry-sipper!
Sauce-preparer,
Pudding-bearer,
Washer-upper –
Need a cuppa?

Sue Cowling

My Dad's Christmas Dinner

I like getting presents,
I like going to dinner.
What do I like about Christmas?
Not when my dad eats sprouts!
My mum bans him from them.

Ella Searle
Aged 7

Mixed-up Mistletoe

I can't understand
why anybody would want to kiss,
especially when you are stood underneath
Mum's middle toe!
Yeeucch!

Christine Gill

You Can See Mary's Knickers!

The shepherds are in line,
The angels dance in time,
Then you hear the teachers cry
You can see Mary's knickers.

The choir followed count,
Christmas cheer is about,
Then the teachers shout
You can still see Mary's knickers.

There were no coffees left on the stall,
That's how the parents got through it all,
Interrupted by the teachers' calls
You'd be blind to miss Mary's knickers!

There was applause and uproar,
Everyone running for the door
They'll never forget what they saw
The sight of Mary's bright pink knickers.

Sally Priddle
Aged 14

Merry Chrismix

Weather crackling.
Sleigh bells humming.
Vicar twinkling.
Robins praying.
Frost photographing.
Holly heating.
Slippers glowing.
Logs glinting.
Candles ringing.
Tinsel playing.
Angels snoring.
Santa baa-ing.
Music unwrapping.
Computers smiling.
Dogs dancing.
Stockings watching.
Presents visiting.
Dad crumbling.
Mince pies dangling.
Grandma barking.
Carol singers shining.
Mulled wine yawning.
Stars warming.
Shepherds hanging.
Sheep flying.
Biscuits raining.
Turkey singing.

La la la

Pudding hopping.
House burning.
Children cooking.

(Unscramble this list of Christmas activities
and then make up your own new version)

John Rice

Remembering Snow

I did not sleep last night.
The falling snow was beautiful and white.
I dressed, sneaked down the stairs
And opened wide the door.
I had not seen such snow before.

Our grubby little street had gone;
The world was brand-new, and everywhere
There was a pureness in the air.
I felt such peace. Watching every flake
I felt more and more awake.

I thought I'd learned all there was to know
About the trillion million different kinds
Of swirling frosty flakes of snow.
But that was not so.
I did not know how vividly it lit
The world with such a peaceful glow.

Upstairs my mother slept.
I could not drag myself away from that sight
To call her down and have her share
The mute miracle of the snow.
It seemed to fall for me alone.
How beautiful the grubby little street had grown!

Brian Patten

The Christmas Confessions of Tom Aged Ten

I'm Joseph in the nativity play
It's horrid and it's scary

But I'm in love with Amanda Binks
And Amanda's being Mary

I've got to wear a stupid beard
It's itchy, smelly, hairy

But I'm in love with Amanda Binks
And Amanda's being Mary

I feel all daft, stuck out on my own
Like a Christmas tree with a fairy

But I'm in love with Amanda Binks
And Amanda's being Mary

I keep forgetting all my words
The teacher's glare is starey

But I'm in love with Amanda Binks
And Amanda's being Mary

The teacher said "Give your wife a hug"
Amanda yelled "How dare he?"

But I'm in love with Amanda Binks
And Amanda's being Mary

Amanda told me to get lost
Her comments did not vary

But I'm in love with Amanda Binks
And Amanda's being Mary

Amanda said that I smell
Like a herd of cows in a dairy

But I'm in love with Amanda Binks
And Amanda's being Mary

Amanda said I make her sick
She said of me, she's wary

But I'm in love with Amanda Binks
And Amanda's being Mary

Yes, I'm Joseph in the nativity play
I hate it and it's scary

But I'm in love with Amanda Binks
And Amanda's being Mary

David Harmer

Snow Joke

Why does it have to be Snowmen?
Why is it never Snowgirls?
Why can't we build a Snow-princess
With berries for rubies and pearls?
Why can't we pick her some holly
And give her a spiky, green crown?
What about icicle diamonds
To wear on her glittering gown?
What about crowds of Snow-ladies
With twiggy and twizzly curls?
Why does it have to be Snowmen?
Why is it NEVER Snowgirls?

Clare Bevan

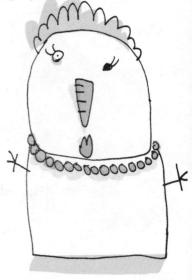

Pantomime Time

We're in our seats.
We've got some sweets.
Just imagine,
we're at Aladdin!
Jewels in a cave,
a princess to save,
a lamp with a genie,
a horrible meanie.
Jokes and songs
and sing-alongs.
We'll have a good time
at the pantomime.

Jill Townsend

behind you....

I Want to be Mary

I want to be Mary.
I know I'd be good.
With a little bit of make-up
I'd look like Mary should.

Don't want to be a shepherd
Or the man at the inn.
Don't want to be a wise man
With a beard on my chin.

I want to be Mary.
But everyone says: "Roy,
You can't be Mary
Because you're a boy!"

John Foster

The Hunt

Oh, rummage and scrummage, rifle and root
Ransack and wardrobe and look for the loot
For the hunt, the hunt
The week-before-Christmas-hunt
Is on!

Prod at the parcels under the tree
That one's for you and this is for me
For the hunt, the hunt
The week-before-Christmas-hunt
Is on!

Search all the cupboards, pick all the locks
Scour through the drawers, shake every box
For the hunt, the hunt
The week-before-Christmas-hunt
Is on!

Jan Dean

Silly Santa Stories

Christmas Limerick

There once was a greedy young elf
who kept Santa's gifts for himself.
He made quite a name
for in time he became
an elf of exceptional welf.

Trevor Parsons

Santa's Last Minute Hitch

He was bang
on schedule
lists sorted
presents packed
and strapped
in the back
of the sledge.
Rolled out of bed
dressed decided
to give his old feet
a last minute rest
wriggled his toes
in his socks
sipped his midnight
mug of tea and was
ready for the "off".

CALAMITY!

"OK," he roared.
*"Which one of you
filled my boot with reindeer pooh?!"*

Patricia Leighton

Santa's Garden

Santa's garden's magic –
You should see the things that grow.
I asked him how he did it,
But he just said, "Hoe, hoe, hoe!"

Marcus Parry

Father UnChristmas

I'm Father UnChristmas
And I curse and I grouse
As I squirm through your keyhole
To de-Santa your house.

I rip up the trimmings,
Break the bulbs in the lights;
In your stocking you'll find
A serpent that bites...
From a time of goodwill
I make a season of fights.

In their boxes, the chocolates
Are turned into stones.
I bring a sack of old worries
And bags of new moans:
From a time of goodwill
I make a season of groans.

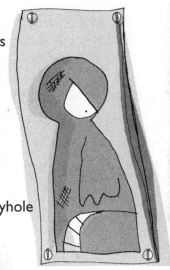

I'm Father UnChristmas
And I curse and I grouse
As I squirm through your keyhole
To de-Santa your house.

Trevor Millum

What Suits Santa

I am the elfin cobbler
And I make Santa's boots.
My sister makes his bobble hats,
My brother makes his suits.

And every year he shows him suits
In colours from yellow to blue.
And every year, Old Santa says
"I think the red will do!"

It used to puzzle me greatly,
But now, no mystery remains.
When scoffing mince pies and sherry,
Red doesn't show the stains.

Ian Larmont

Santa Is A Biker Now

Santa's got a helmet on
and rides a Harley Davidson
since Rudolph (with his nose so bright)
sneezed and set his beard alight.
He's sold his sleigh and bought instead,
a shiny sidecar painted red,
stuffed with presents large and small,
surprisingly, enough for all.
Children, sleepless in their rooms
hear, not bells, but revs and vrooms,
then rush to windows shouting, "Wow!
Santa is a biker now."

Marian Swinger

Santa's Really Bad

It isn't known across the world
by any mum or dad,
that for 364 days a year
Santa's really bad!

His bedroom's so untidy,
he never eats his greens
and underneath that big red suit
Santa rarely ever cleans.

He never likes to blow his nose
and will not wipe his feet,
he doesn't use a knife and fork
when it's time to eat.

So that if you're ever told at all
that Santa won't come if you're bad,
don't believe a word of this
from any mum or dad!

Andrew Collett

The Excitement of Christmas Eve

Too Excited

Tonight I'm too excited
To try and get to sleep
Mum and Dad have told me
To try by counting sheep
Instead I'm counting reindeer
Their noses glowing red
Each one I count just makes me
More wide awake instead
The more I count the closer
Santa seems to be
And I just love the magic
And the mystery

Chris Massey

Written in Soot

I drowsed and dreamt a merry laugh
upon the midnight breeze,
saw Santa in his magic sleigh
dash through the winter frieze,
red baubles hung in reindeer horns
like flying apple trees.

I saw the reindeers dodge and lurch,
while Santa grabbed his sack.
I'm sure I heard old Rudolph shriek –
"Boss, hang on to your hat".
A shadow skimmed the chimney pots
and startled next-door's cat.

I wasn't sure if I had been
asleep or wide awake,
but come the dawn, Dad's sherry glass
stood empty by the grate.
Mum's pies had gone, a sooty thumb
imprinted on her plate.

Celia Gentles

Wishful Thinking

Night sky peppered with stars,
earth dry-iced with moonshine,
pencil-black branches bearing
   pom-poms of snow.

Windows mantled by magic,
candle flames like butterfly wings,
church bells licking darkness
   with silver tongues.

Midnight busy with promise,
excited children panda-eyed and
sleepless, Christmas Day lurking
   round the corner.

Moira Andrew

Reindeer Rap

Well, it's Christmas Eve,
December 24th,
And we're on our way down
From the far, far north.
We got Santa in the sleigh
With a load of Christmas cheer,
We'll deliver the presents
Santa's worked on all year,
So if you think you hear a noise
When you're tucked up in bed,
A sorta scritch-scritch-scratching
Up above your head,
If you hear somebody tapping
Way up there on your roof
It'll just be the pawing
Of a reindeer hoof!
We'll be rapping on the rooftop,
We'll be rapping on the floor,
We'll be rapping on the window,
We'll be rapping on the door!
It's no problem towing Santa
Through the dark and snowy skies
But when he's drinking sherry wine
And eating all those mince pies
We get bored and lonely
And we wanna let him know
There's still a job to do –

96

Hey, man, we really gotta go!
No offence to all you people,
Just a word in your ear –
Maybe you could leave some carrots
For his cool REIN-DEER!
Or
We'll be rapping on the rooftop,
We'll be rapping on the floor,
We'll be rapping on the window,
We'll be rapping on the DOOR!

Sue Cowling

Christmas Eve with Warty Witch

Instead of my stocking,
I've hung up my bat.
I'll enjoy watching Santa
try filling that!

I've left out a glass
of "medicine" tonight.
If he takes a swig
he'll run all through the night…

There's a fire in the hearth
if he comes in that way –
and my pet tarantula
will be waiting to play!

I've arranged for No Parking
on all of the roofs –
and when he gets back to Rudolph
… there'll be clamps on his hooves.

Trevor Millum

I Can't Wait For Christmas

I can't wait for Christmas
Only 125 more days to go
I hope we're going to Granny's this year
And I hope it's going to snow!

I can't wait for Christmas
Only 68 more days to go
I've made my list from the Argos catalogue
What more do they need to know!

I can't wait for Christmas
Only 24 more days to go
We've put up the decorations
Including the mistletoe!

I can't wait for Christmas
Only 1 more day to go
I bet I can't sleep at all tonight
'Cos it's Christmas day tomorrow!

I can't wait for Christmas
Only 365 more days to go.
I know it's a long time to wait
But I do love Christmas so!

Emma Walker
Aged 10

The Christmas Reindeer

From the shadows of the forest
beneath the spiny firs,
in deep December snows
the Christmas reindeer stirs.
He tiptoes to a clearing
to dance, as if to say:
Be glad, join in my carol;
it's almost Christmas Day!

Judith Nicholls

The Magic of Christmas Morning

All For Me!

Big boxes, small boxes,
Underneath the tree!
All of them, I'm hoping,
Are waiting there for me!
For me, for me, for me,
Are waiting there for me!

Guy Borrowdale
Aged 9

Dad's Christmas Morning

2.00 a.m.
It might be exciting, it might be fun
But I'm still sleeping, I'm not done
With yawning and snoring, so off you go
When Santa's been I'll let you know!

3.00 a.m.
It might be fantastic, it might be a thrill
But you woke me up and I feel ill
With lack of sleep, you little so-and-so
When Santa's been I'll let you know!

4.00 a.m.
Now listen here sunshine, get this straight
It's four in the morning, not half-past eight
Just hold your horses, steady up, whoa
When Santa's been I'll let you know!

5.00 a.m.
No he hasn't been yet, just go away
I know he hasn't been yet whatever you say
I think he's got lost in Spain or Mexico
When Santa's been, I'll let you know!

5.15 a.m.
For goodness sake, give me a break
I haven't slept yet, been kept awake
By all this chattering to and fro
When Santa's been, I'll let you know!

Five thirty, NO! Five forty NO!
Five fifty NO! Six o'clock NO!
NO! NO! NO!!!!!!!!!!!!!!!!!!!!!!
When Santa's been, I'll let you know!

8.30 a.m.
Right, let's get up. What's this I see?
You're all asleep, snoring peacefully
I'm off back to bed, I'm lying low
When you think Santa's been, let me know!

David Harmer

103

Christmas Present

Wrote my Christmas letter to Santa
In the leafy month of June
If you want a football for Christmas
You can never write too soon.

I pestered my sister every day;
"Do you think my football will come?"
She shrugged and told me to ask my dad
And Dad said, "Ask your mum."

Oh the months they crawl like snails it seems
And there's hundreds of hours in each day
So I wrote two more letters just in case
My first had gone astray.

But finally Christmas Eve came round
And I tried not to fall asleep
While over the houses and hedges and streets
The snow lay soft and deep.

It was dawn on Christmas morning
When I raised my sleepy head
And saw my football nestling
At the bottom of the bed.

On the roof the sound of reindeer hooves
Cantering over the snow
And the voice of an old man singing,
"Here we go, here we go, here we go."

Gareth Owen

Noelectricity

HUGE disappointment.
My best present is worthless
without batteries.

Ted Scheu

My Favourite Part of my Favourite Day

Un-
block-
ing
my
lumpy
stock-
ing.

Liz Brownlee

Warmest Greetings

It's Christmas morning
And we've planned
To leave our footprints
In the sand;
To picnic barbecue once more
And eat our luncheon by the shore.
The presents from our Christmas tree
We'll open up, beside the sea.
Relaxing in the scorching sun,
We'll play some party games, then run
To cool off in the water clear –
We get a suntan EVERY year!

Here, winter snows are out of reach –
We're Christmassing on BONDI BEACH!

Trevor Harvey

My Pets' Christmas Morning

Lightning my guinea pig has a big pink stocking
In the stocking is a friend called Thunder

My rabbit Fudge has a small purple stocking
Full of chocolate chip carrots

Hammy my Hamster has a tiny red stocking
With a silver cage and a golden wheel

My mouse Pip has a teeny white stocking
With a teeny square of yellow cheese with holes

Rover the dog has a huge brown stocking
With ten tasty sausages

Serefina my cat has a medium gold stocking
With five little balls of sparkly string
And fifteen sugar mice

Daisy Cookson
Aged 5

An Old-fashioned Christmas Present

"They get too much for Christmas."
said Gran, "It's really shocking.
In my young day you got
a few nuts in your stocking,
an orange and an apple
and a hanky from your aunt
and you were grateful for it
unlike modern kids who aren't."
So we put apples in her stocking,
as many as we could fit
and was she grateful for it?
No, she wasn't, not a bit.

Marian Swinger

Boxing Day Blues and Christmas Thank Yous

Christmas Cinquain Thank You

Thanks Gran
Loved the pink rose
Scented bubble bath and
Perfume, shame you forgot I'm your
Grandson

Chris Massey

Some Thank You Letters

Dear Auntie Prue
just thanking you
for the insect repellent.
Really, really excellent!
From now on
I can guarantee
there'll be
no flies on me!

And dear Auntie Dot
this is to let you know
I safely got
the box of tissues.
Thanks a lot.
Our mummy's a case!
She said they should wipe
the smile off my face!

Dear Uncle Ted,
I'm writing this in bed
with a very sore head:
the puzzle you sent
as a Christmas present
just filled my poor brain
with horrible pain.

Matt Simpson

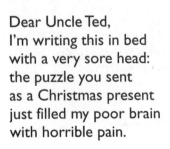

Dear Santa Claus...

Thank you
heaps for
all the
nice presents you
kindly delivered to our door.

You must be so tired
obviously you need to rest
until next Christmas Eve.

Lisa Watkinson

Computerized Christmas Thank You Letter

(Insert/delete as required)

………../……………./200?

Dear (blank)
Many thanks for the (object) received
What a *useful/unusual/lovely/ace/terrific/nice* gift.
I was *over the moon/lost for words/so very pleased*.
It's *just what I wanted/the best thing I had/the
  bee's knees*.

I hope that you *had a good time/a freak out/a rest*.
I was *sad not to see you/thinking about you/spaced
out – you guessed!*
Perhaps when you've *recovered/come round/have
  the time*
You'll *pay us a visit/slam in for a session/drop us a
  line*.

Christmas here was *just brilliant/a scream/the
biggest bore*.
Mum *excelled herself/sends her best wishes/dropped
the turkey on the floor*.
Dad was *his usual self/a real hoot/on top of his form*
And the cat was *so cute/a right menace/out on all
  paws*.

114

Well, I really must *go/finish now/say goodbye/close the prog.*
I have to get *ready for bed/meet the gang/walk the dog.*
Thanks again/I'm so grateful/At last I've finished this letter!
I hope that next Christmas will be *just as good/mega/better.*

Happy New Year.

Kindest regards/Best wishes
Love/Love and kisses
Cheerio/Yo!

(N.B. You are advised to keep a copy of this letter so that you don't send the same one next year!)

Patricia Leighton

Dear Auntie Jane

I can't write you a thank-you-for-my-Christmas-
   present letter
because I have broken my arm/glasses/brain.
My writing paper has been
stolen by Santa
eaten by an aquarium of terrapins
lost in the annals of time
shredded to small pieces in the washing machine.

Frosty the Snowman has leaked all the ink out of
   my only pen
and I have to get the huge dark blue spreading
   stain
out of the cream and white carpet and matching
   settee
before Dad comes home for his tea
(or else).

My second best pencil has mysteriously broken in
   two
my first best, best pencil the hamster has chewed
The Christmas Tree Fairy has posted all the
crayons in the video
there's nothing left to write with although

I could use the computer but it keeps having
   crashes

and the printer prints #@$^*% and sparks
snowflake-type flashes.
So Dear Auntie Jane I would love to write thank
you,
– even though you've forgotten I'm a boy and not
two
and I hate Barbie and pink things – but I can't.
Because I don't have a stamp. Lots of love, Dan.

Lesley Marshall

The Day After

I'm sitting inside and I'm feeling grey –
what an awful boring, raining Boxing Day.
The sweets are all gone, the chocolates too –
there's nothing left to nibble, nothing left to chew.

I wonder if the Wise Men felt the same
waiting in the stable in the pouring rain.

I'm hanging around like the Christmas Star.
My sparkle's fading fast, think I shone too far.
I've opened all my presents, played with all my toys.
Everyone's asleep and I can't make any noise.

I wonder if the shepherds felt this way
sitting in the stable on that Boxing Day.

I'm stuck to the floor and I'm looking mean –
I want to feel like Christmas Eve, red and gold and
    green.
I want to fly around the tree and sit upon the top,
to wave my magic wand and turn back all the
    clocks.

I wonder if the angel felt this bored
after he'd proclaimed the coming of the Lord.

Celia Gentles

Dear Auntie Judith

Dear Auntie Judith,
Thanks a lot
For all the presents that I got:
The tie is nice (likewise the scarf)
The *Simpsons* shorts sure make me laugh –
I only hope you liked *my* gift –
The perfume – though I know it whiffed
A bit, it wasn't cheap,
It cost a quid down Market Street.

Colin West

December 26

A BB gun.
A model plane.
A basketball.
A 'lectric train.
A bicycle.
A cowboy hat.
A comic book.
A baseball bat.
A deck of cards.
A science kit.
A racing car.
A catcher's mitt.
That's my list
of everything
that Santa Claus
forgot to bring.

Kenn Nesbitt

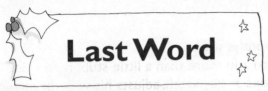

Last Word

The Day After The Day After Boxing Day

On the day after the day after Boxing Day
Santa wakes up, eventually,
puts away his big red suit and wellies,
lets Rudolph and the gang out into the meadow,
then shaves his head and beard.

He puts on his new cool sunglasses,
baggy blue Bermuda shorts (he's sick of red),
yellow stripy t-shirt that doesn't quite cover his
    belly
and lets his toes breathe in flip-flops.

Packing a bucket and spade,
fifteen tubes of factor twenty sun-cream
and seventeen romantic novels,
he fills his ipod with the latest sounds,
is glad to use a proper suitcase instead of the old
    sack
and heads off into the Mediterranean sunrise,
enjoying the comforts of a Boeing 747
(although he passes on the free drinks).

Six months later,
relaxed and more than a little stubbly,
he looks at his watch, adjusts his wide-brimmed
   sun hat,
mops the sweat from his brow and strokes his
   chin
wondering why holidays always seem to go so
   quickly.

Paul Cookson

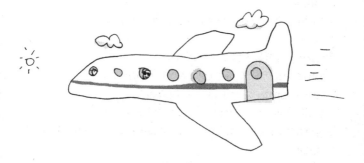

Acknowledgements

The compiler and publisher would like to thank the following for permission to use copyright material in this collection. The publishers have made every effort to contact the copyright holders but there are a few cases where it has not been possible to do so. We would be grateful to hear from anyone who can enable us to contact them so that the omission can be corrected at the first opportunity.

Moira Andrew for "Wishful Thinking".
Leo Aylen for "Remember to Wrap the Presents".
David Bateman for "My Mince Pies (Keep Off)".
Clare Bevan for "Snow Joke".
Guy Borrowdale for "All For Me!".
Liz Brownlee for "Christmas Alphabet" and "My Favourite Part of my Favourite Day".
Richard Caley for "A Christmas Riddle" and "Turkey Surprise".
James Carter for "Christmas Tree".
Andrew Collet for "Santa's Really Bad".
Bill Condon for "Silent Nightmare".
Daisy Cookson for "My Pets' Christmas Morning".
Paul Cookson for "Take Note", "Chrismixed-up Mum", "Family Christmas Scene" and "The Day After the Day After Boxing Day".
Sam Cookson for "Things I Don't Want to Meet Under the Mistletoe".
Sue Cowling for "Reindeer Rap" © Sue Cowling from *Ready, Steady, RAP!* pub. Oxford University Press, 2001, "WANTED" © Sue Cowling from *A Mean Fish Smile* pub. Macmillan, 2000, and "Festive Question".
Jan Dean for "The Shepherd's Story", "Dear Santa", "Mixed

Feelings" and "The Hunt".

Gina Douthwaite for "After-dinner Sleep".

Suzanne Elvidge for "Christmas Dinner".

John Foster for "Who Was There?" and "I Want to be Mary".

Celia Gentles for "Written in Soot", first broadcast BBC Radio
Merseyside, and "The Day After".

Christine Gill for "Mixed-up Mistletoe".

Mary Green for "Crackers!".

Janet Greenyer for "Christmas Crackers".

David Harmer for "Dad's Christmas Morning" and "The
Christmas Confession of Tom Aged 10".

Trevor Harvey for "Warmest Greetings" © Trevor Harvey
from *Poetry Corner 2*, pub. BBC Publications, 1993, and "Some
Truthful Answers to Well-Known 'Mottos' Found in Christmas
Crackers".

David Horner for "Dear Santa".

Mike Johnson for "Christmas Crackers (Cheapo Selection
Box)".

Clare Kirwan for "Home-made Cards".

Ian Larmont for "What Suits Santa".

Patricia Leighton for "Santa's Last Minute Hitch" and
"Computerized Christmas Thank You Letter".

Rupert M Loydell for "Christmas is Coming" and "Sing a Song
of Christmas".

Lesley Marshall for "Dear Auntie Jane".

Chris Massey for "Too Excited" and "Christmas Cinquain
Thank You".

Kevin McCann for "Christmas".

Trevor Millum for "Christmas Stuffing", "Father UnChristmas"
and "Christmas Eve with Warty Witch".

Frances Nagle for "Welcome Note".

Kenn Nesbitt for "December 26" © Kenn Nesbitt from *The
Aliens have landed at our School*, pub. Meadowbrook Press, 2001,

and "Dear Santa, Here's My Christmas List".

Judith Nicholls for "Stable Song" © Judith Nicholls from *Magic Mirror,* pub. Faber & Faber, 1987, and "The Christmas Reindeer" © Judith Nicholls from *Storybox* magazine, 2005.

Gareth Owen for "Saturday Night at the Bethlehem Arms" © Gareth Owen from *The Poetry Store* pub. Hodder Wayland, 2005, and "Christmas Present".

Marcus Parry for "Santa's Garden".

Trevor Parsons for "A Christmas Booklist" and "Christmas Limerick".

Brian Patten for "Remembering Snow".

Peggy Poole for "Something to Play With".

Sally Priddle for "You Can See Mary's Knickers!".

John Rice for "Merry Chrismix" © John Rice from *Guzzling Jelly with Giant Gorbelly* pub. Macmillan, 2004.

Coral Rumble for "Nativity in 20 seconds" © Coral Rumble from *Breaking the Rules* pub. Hodder Wayland, 2004.

Ted Scheu for "Please Don't", "Barely Worth It" and "Noelectricity".

Ella Searle for "My Dad's Christmas Dinner".

Matt Simpson for "Some Thank You Letters".

Roger Stevens for "Deck the Halls" and "Star Worms".

Marian Swinger for "An Old Fashioned Christmas Present" and "Santa Is A Biker Now".

Lynne Taylor for "Christmas Wish" and "Christmas Tingle".

Jill Townsend for "Pantomime Time".

Philip Waddell for "What Christmas is for" and "Six Economy Christmas Crackers".

Emma Walker for "I Can't Wait for Christmas".

Lisa Watkinson for "Dear Santa Claus…" and "Family Get-together".

Clive Webster for "What a Lovely Party", "Drawback" and "Christmas Dinner".

Colin West for "Reggie" and "Dear Auntie Judith".
Kate Williams for "Christmas Baubles".
Neville Ambrose Xavier for "O, Merry Be, Both One And All".